BETWEEN SENTIMENT
AND SENSATION:
Women's Writing Project, Vol. 1

Poetry by

Donna-Marie Riley
Marlena Bontas
Jasmine Gui
Tatevik Khurshudyan

Edited by

Stephanie Bryant Anderson

Red Paint Hill Publishing
www.redpainthill.com

Cover photo: Takeda, Sharon Sadako and Kaye Durland Spilker. Fashioning Fashion: Deux Siècles de Mode Européenne, 1700-1915. Paris: Arts Décoratifs; Los Angeles: Los Angeles County Museum of Art; Munich; New York: Delmonico Books-Prestel, 2013. http://www.lacma.org

Layout & Design: Stephanie Bryant Anderson

Published by Red Paint Hill Publishing
Clarksville, TN 37040

ISBN: 978-0991553853

Table of Contents

Donna-Marie Riley
   bio

         Brave Thing

         Re-write

         Knees

         REM Sleep

         What Happens

         The Holy Word

         Apocalypse

         Love Included

         For Bianca

         Folding Paper

         We Meet Again

Marlena Bontas
   bio

         Sunday's yellow yolk

         The destruction of birds

         Ghost

         Tenuous

         Forever vertical

         One

         Newborns

         Word flow

         Black, early morning

Moonlight, Daylight

Deaf

Jasmine Gui

bio

At Lakeshore

Inpatience

Breathturn

So Beautiful, You Are

The Memory Tree

Wallflower

Upon Meeting My Reflection on the Train

Fruit of the Spirit

Early June

If my Lover was the Sky

There is an Hour that Sounds like Rain

The Day I Died

Wildflower Thoughts

Tatevik Khurshudyan

bio

The Dead Bird

Special Breakfast

Undertone Lullaby

Papers (a day in need of ink)

Text Analysis

MEMORY

William Butler Yeats

One had a pretty face,
and two or three had charm,
but charm and face were in vain,

because the mountain grass
cannot but keep the form
where the mountain hare has lain.

Donna-Marie Riley

Don't ever bow your head
to someone willing to cut it off.

Donna-Marie Riley is a young poet still high off the publication of her first collection *Love and Other Small Wars,* published by Words Dance. Poetry is very much her means of survival; it's what evolves out of a need to understand, express, recover, *endure.* Though she is still finding her voices (note: plural), she is constantly grateful for the opportunities that have been afforded to her, including this one. She'd like to think that writing poetry is similar to building houses: you create something people can live in and you let them call it *home.*

Brave Thing

She says *it's a brave thing, being loved by you*. I don't ask why. I kiss her on her head for her courage. I gold-star her abdomen with my mouth. I leave one hand inside her. Some days, she gets solemn. Some days, she turns the radio off in the kitchen just as I'm getting into a rhythm making omelettes. Some days, she opens and closes the fridge in an attempt to discover where the light goes. She's right. It's a brave thing being loved by me, but then it's a brave thing being loved at all. Where do we find the nerve? We say *all right, I like you, so I put my happiness in your hands*. We say *your smile tickles me so let's spend forever going to bed mad at one another*. Okay, so it isn't always like that. Some people know better. Some people. But not you and I. You and I both keep drunk-driving into new relationships. Keep licking the envelope of someone's mouth. Keep filling the void in our ribcage with whatever we can find. You and I weren't born smart. We were born screaming. I know, I know – aren't we all? Well, sure, but for most of us, it's audible. Anyway, back to what's important:

–

Sorry, I lost my train of thought. I plumed the depths and came up with nothing. Maybe your thighs. Maybe I want to get lost between them. But it isn't all sexual, I promise. Some of it is, but most of it is just – I want to be close to you. Forget waking up next to you. I want to wake up inside you. I'll kiss you morning breath and all. I'll start every day ironing the tension out of your body. Doesn't that sound nice? How domestic. And I've never been that kind of woman. Man. I don't know really. I've never been that person, wanting only to serve another, but god, I want to bring you breakfast in bed. God, I want to bring you to orgasm. It's all the same to me.

Yes, there are times I'm going to hurt you with silence. Yes, there are times I'm going to hurt you with words. I know what you mean. It's a brave thing, being loved by me.

But it's an honour - that you think I'm worth the risk.

Re-write

So okay, I've written this poem before. I've walked through
the backdoor and found him inside another woman.
Now I write her anaconda,
jaw unhinging, and him inside her, twitching.

I haven't used
this metaphor before, but it's the same story.
It's always the same story.
Every three chapters, I pack my bags, dresses first because
I will need them at all the bars I'm destined for the moment I
        close the door behind me.

The door doesn't close behind me. The door mocks me
from, well, the doorway. Sneers at me. Is wooden in its
superiority.
                (Ha. Do you get it? Wooden. Because it's a door.
                But then, I suppose the door could be made of
                something else. Still. It's a joke. Laugh. Laugh if you get
                a joke.
                        Laugh if the blood keeps coming.)

Anyway, you've read this poem before. I'm sorry. I've tried
to stop writing it. I've tried to stop going to bed with it,
but the poem is a great temptress.
The poem learned to belly-dance in Goa. The poem
        kisses like a closed fist. I happen to like that.

        So he calls me on the telephone, except not really,
because this is the 21st century, and no one has telephones
anymore.
                But he calls me on the telephone, real vintage kind,
                avocado green and built into the kitchen wall,
                20 ft of wire.
                        I can hear him frying bacon while he apologizes.

He says, "It wasn't about you, it wasn't my idea, it wasn't
a choice."

And I say, "I know. I know it wasn't about me.
                    Remember to turn the bacon."

And there is a sound of metal scraping something else,
whatever pans are made of, and then he says, "Thanks, I knew
you'd understand, I knew you wouldn't blame me."

                 "Of course not," I say,
       "I don't blame you."

"Good,"
      he says,
             "good."
                    and I say,

"I've got to go now. I've got to go.
       I'm laughing, but the blood keeps coming."

Knees

Today you are wearing a dress that shows your knees and I want to apologize to your knees for all the grovelling other people have made them do. I want to say, 'I'm sorry, knees, I'm sorry they made you kneel at their feet and make excuses for the body you belong to.' You do not have to make excuses. Your body is a surprise party that made me trap my hand in the doorframe. Your body made me spit up all my beer. Your body made me stupid. It's just so… unexpected. Your body: a curve in the road that leads a person to their destiny. Please don't ever get down on your knees again. Please don't ask them to love you. Love is not something you ask for. Help getting the spices down from the top shelf is something you ask for. Extra cheese on your cheesy fries is something you ask for. More time is something you ask for. Love is something that is given. A non-returnable gift at the surprise party of your body. I laid it on the table of your heart. The surprise party is for me, but I got something for you for being such a good host. Here, I got you this love swelling into something almost worrying. No take backs. Here, this is for you. This is for being so… unexpected. Don't ever fall to your knees again. Don't ever kiss someone's feet for a fraction of their affection. Don't ever bow your head to someone willing to cut it off. Wear dresses every day. I love your knees. I love the body they belong to. 'Surprise!' and all the lights go on. 'Surprise!' and my mouth falls open.

REM *Sleep*

In some of the dreams you turn all the lights out. Use only a
flashlight to shadow a bunny rabbit on my bedroom wall. You're
happy sometimes. When your eyes go bright I want to read fairy
tales to your left foot. I want to leave the wolf out of the story. I
want your laugh inscribed on my gravestone. Call me morbid.
Call me a romantic. Just call me, sweetheart. The phone rings
and it's not you. The phone rings and they're turning the gas off.
The phone rings and my sister is pregnant. The phone rings and
I didn't get the job. The phone rings and—nothing. Is it you?
Did you get lonely? Did you forget that you hate me? It's okay. I
can swallow that knife. I was raised Circus. I want to tightrope
your spine. I want to jump through the hoop of your mouth. I
promise never to raise a whip to your lions.

Hey, in some of the dreams you're crying sometimes. You realize
what a terrible mistake you've made and get my shirt all wet.
That's all right—about the shirt, I mean. I spilled ketchup on it
anyway. (I didn't really spill ketchup on it.) Anyway, I like you
like this too. Your sad puppy face. A moon in each cheek. Hair
stuck to your temples. It's gorgeous—the way you exist. How do
you do it? Let's notify Cosmo. 101 Ways to Knock a Guy Out.

1. Wear pajamas in the daytime.

13. Sing badly.

27. Tongue kiss his heart.

54. Laugh as much as you cry.

55. Cry as much as you love him.

99. Let him help you.

100. Let him try at least.

The list goes on. The list is endless. In some of the dreams, I'm running. The faster I run, the longer the distance becomes. Like in a bad suspense movie when the hallways stretch ahead of you while you're trying to outrun the serial killer. Or trying to get to the bathroom. I'm trying to get to you. The hallways stretch. Your silhouette gets smaller. My voice won't work. I can't yell for you. I can't run fast enough. And of course I trip on absolutely nothing. The floor rises up to meet me, there's a sound like cracking knuckles but louder, the breath gets caught in my chest, you're still tiny in the distance, there's blood on the floor,

I wake up

and I wake up

and I wake up.

What Happens

There is no good way to tell our story.
The sequence of things doesn't matter:
the time you kissed me spineless;
touching each other underwater in an attempt
to drown our desire;
your heart as large and holy as a cathedral and me
praying for salvation.

It doesn't matter.

What matters is that your mouth
appeared to me like a battleground.
Looked like something you never come back from the same.
What matters is that the questions all went unanswered
and your hands collected dust.

Imagine driving into the mouth of a river.
Now imagine not wanting to escape.
That is how you felt to me.

Three weeks after we met in the flesh you said to me
you're not what I was looking for
but you're what found me first.

What happens when the thing you are looking for finally shows
up?
When it wears a button-down shirt and has bony knees.
What happens when it loves you back?
When it has been looking for you too.

I'll tell you what happens:

my face falls into ruin.
my heart gets ground into burger meat.
I lose the battle to your mouth at the
penultimate moment,

and someone else rushes in with a second to spare
and slays it with their tongue.

I'll tell you what happens:

you are left only with scars
and you eat your sadness pink in the middle.

The Holy Word

No.
I have finally learned to say it.
To taste it. To suck it between my teeth.
To let it melt on my tongue, holy bread that it is.
The only real salvation. I push it into
the hands of strangers. The hips of women.
The mouths of men, hanging open like doors
pulled clean off their hinges. I have come so far.
I repeat it into the mirror, my daily mantra:
no, no, no.
I am born again in the power of it.
I can feel my muscles tensing. My eyes
hardening. My body practices its imitation
of a shotgun shell. This is the magic of
self-empowerment. The easiest way
to a revolution.
The government fallen to its knees.
Streets doused in gasoline.
The rise of the masses, suddenly
fully conscious and armed with
the deadliest of weapons: *No!*
It all begins and ends here.
You fold the word into the pages of your
heart. Treat it like a Bible. Quote from it
when they begin the defense.
"No: the only freedom."
You never dreamt it could be like this,
never imagined it was even an option.
You had to learn, had to study the form,
had to immerse yourself in the art of declining
invitations. When yes becomes a noose you
keep hanging yourself with, no is the only
way to keep your feet on the ground.
No becomes the slack in the rope,
becomes the only way to get yourself down
from the ceiling beams. The only way to
get yourself down off the cross.

Apocalypse

Because we've been here so many times, I have stored up on
canned goods and dry cider. By here I mean the metaphorical
end. The fuse of our relationship ran out to where everything
annihilates. Or at least we're told it will. And because we're
always here, because hurricane season is every season, because
your body screams apocalypse every time I touch it, I have taken
certain precautions. Every time you get a little distant, I drag us
both down to the basement of our doubt and make us wait out
the explosions. I kiss the side of your jawline and feed you
sweetcorn seasoned with Chinese five spice. We sleep on old
duvets with the feathers poking out everywhere and you wake up
snapping *I hate geese!* Of course we are unaware of time down
here. All the hours pass much the same: me whispering your
name like a holy chant and the echoes giving you goose bumps.
I'd tell you I love you but that's too obvious and won't change
anything. Instead of that, I sleep poorly without you. I lose
weight without trying. I listen to my heartbeat and it mentions
your blue sundress. Instead of I love you, I don't. Said with all
the conviction in the world and still no one believes me. We've
been here so many times before. We're depleting all the
resources. Down to the last can of tuna. Down to the final burst
of try. I'll let you have the last of both and won't resent you for a
minute.

Love Included

i.

A photograph frayed at the edges. You leaning into the sun,
leaning out of love, you wear a white dress and you are laughing.

The joke is your hand softly curled around his upper arm;
the joke is his eyes intent on your mouth.

The joke is a private one between two archetypes
of a romance novel:

he has broad shoulders and very green eyes
and you don't mind when your lipstick smudges.

ii.

I am the punchline.

iii.

After that picture was taken, we went home and made love
in the dark, your pupils so enlarged I nearly fell inside them.

I didn't know yet
and you never had.

All things, love included, have the propensity to leave you
starved.

iv.

I spent three months getting rid of all of your things,
as if doing it over a longer period of time meant you
somehow left me slower.
Or that there would always be something to bring you back.

As if one day you'd remember your purple hairbrush.
Or your silk nightgown. Or my shaking hands.

Like you couldn't just get a new hairbrush from the supermarket.
Like your body wouldn't make any man tremble.

v.

It took a long time to get here.
I have learned to be kinder to myself. To stop conflating my
self-worth
with your leaving.

To accept the loneliness when it comes, and to be thankful when
it doesn't.

All things, love included, are thrown in the fire eventually.

For Bianca

Of all things, I lose my voice most often. I imagine it sometimes,
a slow spill down the side of your bed. An old vinyl suddenly
going silent as you touch me. A candle flickering out of
existence. In secret, I imagine you. The heavy dusk of your skin.
Your eyes prehistoric in their sadness. Your smile a sliver of
moonlight. I spend time considering your body. Think mostly of
softness. Of warmth. Of losing my hands. You are slow in my
mind. Measure every decision carefully, could spend all your life
deciding whether or not to love me. And I'd wait all the while,
collect cherry blossoms from the garden and leave them under
your pillow. Thread sprigs of lavender through all your
buttonholes. Watch the television on mute. Tell the neighbours
you aren't well when they ask to come for dinner. Bianca, I
imagine you gentle. Generous. Well-spoken. I imagine you know
what to do with lonely girls who have small hands. Imagine you
might have been one yourself before the calmness came. Before
the deep breaths and self-reflection. Before the prolonged and
much-needed silence. I have built you in my head out of
sunflower seeds and violins. Hazelnut and goose feathers. Warm
milk and laundry softener. I have built you out of your good
name and my sweet tooth. And I imagine again my voice, this
time summoned from my throat by the calling of your blood.

Folding Paper

It's winter so the sun is low.
It's winter so we are crying over spilled milk.

I wish the past had taken yoga.
Wish it had that flexibility.

What if we could make
origami out of our childhoods?
I'd make yours a lotus flower.
Float it down a river that never
ends in waterfall.

I had a dream about you in a field of violets.
You were turning like a spinning top.

I yelled something like *I love you*
into the eye of your tornado
except I tend to avoid the actual words
so it came out
you make me heart-sore.

It's true anyway—
you make me feel like the after tinge
of a dirty punch.

Everything throbbing.
A headache in the bridge of my nose.
I can't stop pulsing.
I can't look into the light.

Which reminds me – you're full of it.
I've never spent so much time shielding my eyes.
I've never played the part of Icarus
with quite as much conviction.

About the origami –
I'd make mine a paper crane.
Let you turn my wings to ash.

We Meet Again

in an empty book shop. No, in a field of violets. At a farmer's
market down South when the heat has broken like an eggshell.
Your hair is longer. Shorter. Dyed bright purple. Still the same.
We meet again by chance at a New York City bus stop. You
have exact change. I wink at the driver. We meet again in
February when the snow is so tired of itself it melts into the
pavements like a slow yawn. We meet again at a poetry club in
the heart of some small town in England. You sip at a beer.
Keep your legs crossed. Find my eyes in the corner, two
pinpricks in the distance. Fairy lights around a fireplace. We
meet again after the in-between years. We're older. You look it. I
hear your voice over the intercom in a railroad station. I catch
your scent in the aisle of a supermarket. We meet again at the
feet of the Eiffel Tower. Neither of us impressed. No, both of
us swollen with awe. Your camera frames me before you even
notice. We meet again in the middle of the ocean. No, under a
bridge in Mexico. No, in the shadow of a skyscraper. Under the
scope of a comet. At the edge of the universe. Before the end of
the world. We meet again at a party. Leave together. Make love
until we turn to salt. Until we are nothing but steam rising in a
windowless room. Until we remember what tore us apart to
begin with. We meet again at the brink of a climax. No, at the
root of a toothache. In the hollows of your collarbone. We meet
again at the height of our loneliness. Part again when it comes
back.

Marlena Bontas

He'll eat your soup
and sleep in your bed.

He'll wear your socks,
and say nothing to you.

An avid reader, Marlena Bontas is a cynical observer of love and the world around, but most of the time a forgivable one who likes to play with the fire of her feelings and get burnt. In her home country, Romania, she published a small collection of poetry and a journalistic essay in 2006/2008.

Marlena fell in love with Sylvia Plath at a late age and now she's addicted to her words. She doesn't have children but she considers her poems, her adopted children, because they don't belong to her, her poems come from far away, a place she doesn't know yet but she hopes she will someday....with a little help from writing and psychotherapy.

Sunday's yellow yolk

The yolk of the sun
is sizzling in the pan.
it hardens at the sides and,
as it fries,
the light that came through the window
blacks out.

I taste it when it's ready
but it's difficult to eat
the bones of the life
I wanted to live,
as I imagined.

The destruction of birds

He plucks the feathers of a boiled chicken
over a bucket of water,
showing me how to do it and,
if I learned, he'll be happy with me.

I listen to him,
And watch him
like I'd watch a star at night
Falling towards me.

He guards his wine glass sitting on the table nearby
while talking to me,
like he was talking to a stranger in the street.

Unbuttoning his shirt, he then falls heavily in the sofa
knowing how to look at me from under the grey
eyebrows that
weigh down on his eyes.

And then he says something significant
So I think it must be the end of the world
or some sort of discussion about love
and forgiveness-
He says they're unrelated.

Ghost

Bitter thoughts wrap themselves
around me
biting from this moment with the only
hunger they possess.

I sit in the backseat and watch
how my heart craves for a way out
of my shirt.

Just like the hares that pass me by,
the cars on the road,
the stars,
and people who drag their feet into the clouds,
I thrive to go somewhere, too
Wishing for the driver to go faster.

Painless and cold like a steel,
or a razor out in the rain,
I shudder at the thought of watching
you cut your face in the mirror.
You're the spitting image of me
or is it the other way around?

And after I left you,
you left me
out there in the open.
You took my clothes, emptied my pockets
of their birds, rainbows and dreams.

When the car stopped, there was nothing I could do.
I was already up there, on the moon,
watching the earth stare at me in wonder.

Tenuous

Sometimes, I let the dream of you
find its way to my bed,
my night bed where I rest and focus
on entering the void
on my own.

The tongues of fire
are flowers covering me
in the garden of your hell.
I don't want to leave a trace behind me,
a small footstep, an earring dropped
in the ash
so you could find me
and eat me with kisses,
with a mouth full of words.

I wouldn't need my hands to hold
the babies of fear crying and twisting
under my breast.
I would be alone with you
on a planet with arms
and feet and everything
in between.

If you found me we'd look like tulips-
red and quiet
like the insides of a dead heart.

Nobody will watch us
or talk about us,
our bodies will hold themselves
in a state of forgiveness.

Nobody will know about our encounter
below the earth level,
ready to enter the eye of god,
to become a blind spot in its madness.

Forever vertical

A cat meows far in the distance,
between the broken elements of winter.
The last dreaming hours
where my head was spinning
and love wore my skin as a coat,
made me shaking and thinking
at something
to keep me warm.

I stumble upon the screaming trees
Watch out!
I beg to get there fast,
painless,
but the blackness in the air keeps
me on spot.

I can't see or move—
my feet have now roots in the ground,
perhaps until love
or death will cut them away.

One

Why is it warm in a room crowded
with people?
Is it because of the thoughts buzzing
in their minds like fireflies?
Because of the words they mutter
to each other,
facing each other like mirrors?

Why is it that only one person
will stand up and come to you,
humble or arrogant
in his discourse on humanity?

Do you think this person
was 'one' before he met you?

Was he alone
with his clothes,
with his names,
with the details of the people
around him?

He'll then open each door
by your side, if you let him
and see the world
as you see the world.

He'll eat your soup
and sleep in your bed.

He'll wear your socks,
and say nothing to you
when you're not around.

The temporary room is
left behind.

Newborns

I am naked but not because of you
and your hands,
not because I forgot my clothes
and went out shameless, in the dark,
sleepwalking to insanity.

I am naked because of
my skin covered in grass
or in leaves that fall only in autumn.
I am naked because someone
asked me to explain why I was born.

I am naked because time is naked ahead
of me,
waiting for me to cease on my own.

I am naked like you
under your clothes,
I am naked like them
with child blood on their hands,
with ice cream melting on their lower lip.

I want to cry like you want to cry
about the world and its undoing
about the houses we left to drown
in our love,
long before our passing.

Word flow

Tell me everything,
for I know nothing.

Tell me about water and why is it wet.
Tell me why elephants aren't green or yellow
like parakeets.
Tell me how electricity works,
and how your boss works for money.

Tell me about the surface of the sun:
will you have dinner with me there?

Tell me about what you don't know
and what I don't know.

Tell me cat stories, rooster stories the ones
that are written at 5 am by underpaid writers.

Tell me how the time works
and what is the time now?

Tell me about planets and galaxies
about ET and IT, what is the difference?
Tell me if you've ever seen a star dying
or a couple of moons coloring
the night sky.

Tell me if you've seen a volcano
and if god can get you out of it if
you decide to jump?
Have you ever owned silver or gold?
Have you ever built a church or thought
of burning one if you had enough money?

Tell me something about me I don't know
something that will surprise me,
something that will make you think about

yourself also,
about who we are in a world that needs two
for survival.

I'll like everything you say
I'll write down every word that sounds better
than the previous
and with each letter I find in your name or in the words
you speak daily,
I'll make acronyms and assume
that you invented the alphabet
just to be able to tell me something,
anything.

Black, early morning

If there's no light,
No mirror to deflect it,
No floating thought
Above the city land,
I'll pack my clothes, my years
And bury my possessions
In litter or in sand.

If there's no more night,

No full moon,
Or dreams of love as dark
Or bright;
If there would be one star,
One candle lit near a window frame,
If there was no more winter,
Rain or
If the sunlight and the moonlight
Were the same,
I'd carry myself
And forget about myself
In this godless,
endless morning.

Moonlight. Daylight

Two bright lights above sea
float like yesterday's thoughts
about you.
Your darkness pushed me in a hole
and I cried like someone else's
child.

I saw little flashes from the dream
I supposed to dream,
from the life I supposed to live
but there was nothing I could do—
you took my arms, my legs
and made from me a saint on a cross,
sucking from each wound what I thought
was the poison of loving the world for too long,
of wanting parts of you like I wanted a tree,
a swan on a lake
or god's eyelashes on my pillow.

I am not a hole in the body so you can
fit in a soul or two,
hours at dawn have passed
until all saints that carried my body
to the sea
did something against your love:
they prayed and hoped that
what you meant for me was only
bad blood on a Christ's leg.

The next day, god became immune
to our reunion.
Then, I shrieked and screamed
when the earth and the moon above us
came as one.

Deaf

Until the gold fields spread unto the streets,
the night streets where darkness lies
as a bum,
until the sun hides and shines no more
where it has to
and our only light is the thought of love
that makes us real and forgiving,
I'll be less than a dream,
a small occurrence of a cry into the night,
petrified by those who sleep
and never hear a thing.

Jasmine Gui

This is how I ground myself:
an hourglass is sand in sand. A ghost is time
in time. A grief is sadness in sadness.
Yesterday is old mirror.
.

Jasmine was born in Singapore, raised in three different cities, and currently lives in Toronto. She began writing as a young person to hold and remember her thoughts and emotions. Moving from city to city, her words glued her life together in cohesive-like pieces, even when external environments and relationships were broken by time and space. Today she continues to write poetry as a way of telling herself things she is otherwise too stubborn to hear, or too prone to forget. It is how she comes to know, and love her selves as she grows in and out of them. Her poems have been published in *The Winter Tangerine Review*, *Acta Victoriana*, *Red Paint Hill*, *(parenthetical)*, and more. You can find her talking to herself at jasminventory.wordpress.com.

At Lakeshore

Somewhere in my dream last night
you step off the bus by lakeshore and dust your jacket
shoulders, an easy smile.

your backpack is full of smooth stones
you pull out, bend and place
one by one side by side
around our feet and count,
fingertips stepping.

So clearly in my dream the creases in your hands
show themselves. The exact shade of dark you are.
the faster we touch, the more each count
crackles until everything flickers.

The lake is on fire too and my memory sinks,
rolling with the tide out to deep water.
So light now, the weight of your
head on mine.
So ashen now, ring of stones.
So charred now, these fingers.

Somewhere in my dream like a leaf
on the crust of lakeshore you fall,
a ripple against ripples.

Inpatience

I wake to a sweater of fog in my skin,
cream wool in my fingers,
a snowbank sky in my veins.
I wake to coating vision and grey pause in my wrists,
habited by the texture of ordinary days.

windowsill sit quiet in your wordless way,
I shall tuck my ears into the soles of my feet.
stillness wrap your hand in mine,
I shall be a cloud on a vanishing street.

today the light of me is impartial,
favours all shadow the same.
and fog knows no other shape of thought
save

       tomorrow I will carry on,
       and today I will stay.

Breathturn

I hear a rowboat docked
in your voice of looking my way.

The wind sweeps hair across my face,
an impatient gesture
I forget when your eyes capsize
between thought lines and my beached toes sandy
with paraphernalia
intent,
cupped oceans.

Early morning is my favourite sweater.

The weather vane catches a seam
on my way (I have pinned
loose hairs with star this time) up
there the darkness unravels naked against my knees,
and finds you
on the dewy horizon, light going its years.

I hear in me sea breeze arrowed
against
the colour in you rising,
understand how our lungs turn breath
in swallows.

So Beautiful, You Are

What if we—
he thinks but never gets further
as Monday morning slides over his feet in sunlit panels
and holds his attention
while elsewhere in the city someone slips
on the sidewalk but doesn't
                    so laughter. Early morning laughter
thinning like dawn mist and
waking eyes.

The leaves wave good day to coffee cup steam in
pearl grey breezes he scratches in
the same lazy bed stretch.
Everywhere the last dregs of calm drain downtown
in sudfoam crests humming
daysdrift dayssleeptillnoon dayscrunchdays mydays
pickuplaundry days
                    —this is
the fifth caffeine cup ring on the wooden table.
little overlapping stains drying out
because daylight. Strong glaring daylight
at midday distilling near windows
in sleepy rest.

He rests toes on the sill to uncurl
with the afternoon.
There was a thought
he remembers but never gets any further,
the day always slips in-between
and holds his attention   so
                    beautiful, you are.

The Memory Tree

She thinks herself in railway weed. Solitary
thought. Other days she is rattling stone.

When the train travels through her veins, for days
all she hears is the root of her teeth rumbling,
feels the dead heat in blood tunnels rising
to stick her tongue to its roof.

There could be a rush of water under her feet,
some days a whole other city might be moving
            ; the pothole is a photograph to listen to.
            ; the pothole is a mouthful of dirt.
            ; the pothole is a pore on the skin.
Under ground, she plants a bunch of tangled
shoelaces growing into trees of leaving
for days. She thinks herself in magnolia
bursting by a station exit, falling
blooms full at her tangling feet.
a speechless rising for days.

There is a browning sweetness about weathered thinks.

Wallflower

Your eyes crack. Wall chips tearbudding
like spring leaves. An uncertain greening.
you say sadness pushes through concrete. Grief takes
root. Tender white roots dig around deadthings.
The rain is a bitter drink. Acid sorrow you say.
The whitewash is a furnace in the day.

They photograph your strength,
your life is miracle they look,
oh brave little wallflower in the city.

But no you never wanted to be a show.
But no you never wanted to be alone.
You whisper for cool earth and shared sunshine.
Yet for the fullness of a meadow
and one fading pink sky smile.

The shadow behind you lengthens into
solitary dark on a midday wall,
they photograph that too.
They are obsessed with haunting you say.

Upon Meeting My Reflection on the Train

Today is to grieve
over certain innocence
in laughter over certain
clarity of sight.   I know—
                      the earth is where
we grow—but
still, there are deaths we die along the way;

my ghosts move between frames
often they emerge in train windows sometimes,
remember him?   Her eyes tease me.
How you loved him.

Ah, these mirrors are hardened sandy planes.
         She coils her hair neatly around fingers
              raveling, unraveling,
         hoods the dunes of her eyes
in curving sand snake print.

I touch my own face when I meet the
apparitions, pretend
the warm flush of skin is a glowing morning.

This is how I ground myself:
an hourglass is sand in sand. A ghost is time
in time. A grief is sadness in sadness.
         Yesterday is old mirror.

Fruit of the Spirit

The city in sunset is the colour of peaches,
yogurt skies I dip a spoon in and
bring to my lips.
Sirens the texture of strawberries swell
against my teeth in evening air
I swallow.

They are quarrelling in the living room.
Gnarly words sprouting from wooden
stake lips. All I focus on
is my steadfast eyelid listening to pain
ripening.

Hello, moonlight. You are the round hardness of a pit.
Hello, evenstar. You are the crown stem of a berry.

The night is dusky mould
growing,
            a darkness I force myself to eat.

Early June

Memories have no power, you said.
It is not my memory that keeps you
waiting but the hope of again, my skin
against your skin someday.
Oh but I said,
What drives this hope if not memory?
The sighing red of your parted lips.
The exact curve of your eyelashed thinking.
And always the steady of your chest
rising and falling in a rhythm I have followed to this
moment. Even my lungs have the hope of memory.
Too, my skin remembers
the folding creases of shirt against cheek
against hair strands
blowsy and undone. It is always June in my head,
and the sun is always setting between your fingers
buried in your laughing. I glance
your way under eyelids heavy for fear of joy. Even
on a yellow wilting August afternoon, even
in the cool darkness of a November moon you are
half curled into the shallow of my lap.
Memory waits with me always in the hope of again
for you.

If my Lover was the Sky

I lick the last smear of sunset from your lip
as you whisper beneath the horizon at highway's end,
a darkening expanse.
Laughter is starshine in your velvet throat
I trace galaxy whorls on,
Dear.

I float with your cloudy sighs
on the back of my breath.
Watching young love on the shoreline
while you murmur pale heaviness
and high tides.

The gravity in your voice keeps me,
Dear.
I stamp your cheeks with nude daylight
while you exhale
over the bare streets of my body
a sunrise.

There is an Hour that Sounds like Rain

When curtains are restless against the open window,
she wraps herself into them
for company.
                        It has always been her way.
Like the time she couldn't sleep
and sat up to watch dawn fall into a fog grey.
The kind unremembered dreams are made of.

Tonight there is none of that though.
Only the winking thunder
above city sleepers and late night minutes painted
            - streetcar -
red interrupting her -
            is there another word for midnight?
She wonders, ten curled toes in bed.
            I would like to embrace this hour by name.
            You are Today.

Elsewhere,
he imagines she uncurls from her sheets
much like spring.
A drowsy sort of extrication.
Thick sleep melting off her shoulders
in folds while she yawns
and stretches into a morning splash of cloud
too wispy to condense into a solid form he can touch.

In his heart's eye
he holds today's memory of her
                        - the steam of her teacup, a
                                    cloudy silhouette -
in a quivering rain splatter sliding down
the windowpane,
            is there another word for memory?
he thinks.
                        it has always been his way.

The Day I Died

The sky was vain and indecisive
the day I died.
Clouds heaped like the pile
of dirty clothes on my bed.
My mudbrown boots on pavement kept time
to my heartbeat as i walked the streets
        growing in different spheres of lost-thought
        pop pop pop at the ambulance wail.
Green shoots of silence in my feet waited
the day I died.
A kind of faithfulness, my feet had.
        (stopped when I stopped for a beautiful end)
the gravel underfoot whispered that day,
and I heard it while falling.
Spring. Spring is wet and scattering,
                they said.
I understood scattering more cleverly,
when I hit the ground and the wet tore my skin open.
In my thoughts
I thought indecisive thoughts;
like what I might have worn to meet death
        (that LBD with the lace detail on top maybe)
and now it is a few splatters too late,
dark veiny leaves are at my feet spreading.
I take my shoes with me. Shoes
the colour of earth after rain.
Their constancy I loved till the end.
They bloomed a poem for the street
the day I died.
They wore me to the grave.
A kind of faithfulness, my feet had.

Wildflower Thoughts

Later, I break the skin of a plum and taste
grace dripping down
my arm. Roll its wood-shell heart around
the white flat of a plate. Later
electrical lines try contemporary
art but the clouds Monet through, while
beneath them I wipe my mouth and
photograph your laughter. Later,
grassy laughter soft on the feet.
I collect your words, ripe
acorns falling into my skirt.
I inhale your fire in dandelion seeds. Later,

we watch the wind take away our skin
and the last crumbs of spring.

The tulip heads are empty,
they gave everything.

Tatevik Khurshudyan

On a paper bed in the corner
I slept with my paper dreams,
after taking off their paper clothes.

Tatevik Khurshudyan was born in 1980, in Ararat, Armenia. She enjoys history, art, nature, literature, good talks, nice people. In 2004, Tatevik won the "best Armenian young poet" award. In 2005, on 21st March, (on International Poetry Day), The Armenian P.E.N. club awarded her second place for her poetry. Khurshudyan's works have been printed in *Grakan Tert, Garoun, Eghitsi Louys*(Armenia), *Taj Mahal Review*(India),*Nouvelles d'Armenie* (France),*Up the Staircase (USA)*, and *The Scruffy Dog Review (USA)* among others. One of the two most important things in her life is her daughter, Beatrice, who Tatevik says, will one day think Tatevik brought her to this world, but really, Beatrice was the one who brought Tatevik here. Second is her pen, the greatest gift from nature and she has to be thankful to it, by writing.

The Dead Bird

There is a dead bird in the middle of road.
Looking out,
I try to imagine its death.
While the rain waltzes with the window frames,
you pour the coffee,
make a kitchen-warm smile with your lips.
You ask me to eat my cake
(*because life will not be cakes every day*, you say,
enjoy it today).
I smile back to you
and eat my piece of cake
with an unending look
to the dead bird.

Special Breakfast

I've mastered this game since my birth
and for almost 25 years
it's so dear to me
to fold up my loneliness
and use it instead of pillow…

I've walked along uneasy pathways
and met men
of different sizes
having different sexual trends…
fooling around…different religions…
Now all of them
are sleeping in the arms of my memories,
and it's of no importance
with whom they are sleeping now,
the only important thing is my blanket
which is perfect and warm enough…

I've learned
to drink my loneliness, as if a cup of natural juice,
since my childhood,
when I was shaking the colored story-books,
believing
that the heroes would pour out
and be a part of a play…

Laid upon the Arabian couch
I'm enjoying le café de Paris,
while thoughts are knocking on the gates of my brain,
reminding that so many men
are thinking of me right now
in different countries,
But I consider each of them as a *joujou*
and go on folding my loneliness,
using it instead of pillow…

Every night
the Night makes love with everyone until dawn,
but here, in my room, he always sleeps

and the boredom flows out
from his shut eyelids
like melted ice-cream…

Every morning
I greet the Time-beggar beneath my window
and I throw my Dream-coins
onto its wet palm

While the same old woman
tries to wash the face of the city
with a bucketful of water,
my stomach starts its usual fight with the world:
it's time for breakfast.

I know the rules of this game so well,
and it's typical for me
to drink my loneliness, as if a cup of natural juice,
at breakfast time,
and, at the same time,
to think about all *joujous*
with a fake smile.

Fr. joujou – toy

Undertone Lullaby

Do you remember
our short, fairytale life
sitting hand in hand at the old fireplace
with woolen socks and warm tea mugs
and happiness
drawn across our faces?

Do you remember
the smell of cakes and meals
in our milk-white kitchen
your dough-covered fingers
and the cookies for Santa
and the carrots for Easter Bunny?

Do you remember
how my little feet
would never fill your high heel shoes
and how I couldn't wait
to grow up quickly?

Do you remember
my colorful dream
of being on stage,
and seeing only your face
among thousands of people,
your diamond tears
sketching a big heart
on your oval face?

Do you remember
when I was sick in bed
smelling of raspberry,
aspirin, honey and sweat,
and when your kiss
was the best comfort?
    (I do remember
    how I always believed
    that your kiss could cure
    any sickness)

Standing here
remembering
your beautiful almond eyes
your perfumed jewelry
and the warmness of your palms
I don't really know
where did all those
joy
meals
cookies
kisses
and laughter
suddenly disappear
And how did your heart freeze
like an early morning window in winter,
And how did we change,
how did we estrange…

Oh, Mother,
could you ever believe
that I would sing you a lullaby
one late night
          from this distance?

Papers (a day in a need of ink)

That unwritten poem became a paper plane
that I threw from the paper window
when paper emotions scattered around the room
and the paper words tried hard to explain
the paper love.

On a paper bed in the corner
I slept with paper dreams,
after taking off their paper clothes.

The poem soared over people made of paper,
who walked down the paper streets,
and finally hung from a bare tree
as an only leaf.

Everything around, made of blank paper.

Text Analysis

Frequency and top words:

Word	Occurrences
you	*171*
your	*116*
love	*28*
time	*25*
our	*19*

Expression	Count	Frequency	Prominence
i	53	0.7%	42.6
me	16	0.2%	55
he	14	0.2%	42.9
want to	14	0.2%	73.7
tell me	13	0.2%	32
i want	13	0.2%	79.7
tell	12	0.2%	32.2
you	12	0.2%	44.7
we meet	11	0.1%	55.8
you are	10	0.1%	39.2
i am	9	0.1%	40.4
meet again	9	0.1%	51.4
i have	9	0.1%	51.7
the same	9	0.1%	57
your body	9	0.1%	75.7
if	6	0.1%	28.9
am naked	6	0.1%	34.5
if you	6	0.1%	42.5
the world	6	0.1%	43.1

to be	6	0.1%	43.2
it is	6	0.1%	46.9
no	6	0.1%	48.7
they	5	0.1%	12.5
my skin	5	0.1%	20.4
she	5	0.1%	23.5
your	5	0.1%	27.2
the sun	5	0.1%	36.1
the last	5	0.1%	36.6
the time	5	0.1%	37.4
you never	5	0.1%	44.4
i wake	5	0.1%	51.7
i imagine	5	0.1%	57.8
i can't	5	0.1%	59
days she	5	0.1%	60.4
for you	5	0.1%	61.8
to you	5	0.1%	67.8
he says	5	0.1%	67.9
i love	5	0.1%	68.4
i know	5	0.1%	77.3

phone rings	5	0.1%	77.9
the phone	5	0.1%	77.9
something you	5	0.1%	79.3
your knees	5	0.1%	81.2
days	4	0.1%	14.4
the city	4	0.1%	15.5
the night	4	0.1%	21.7
an	4	0.1%	24.3
there was	4	0.1%	27.7
and	4	0.1%	28.4
the earth	4	0.1%	28.7
eyes	4	0.1%	30.3
bed	4	0.1%	31.6
hands	4	0.1%	37.4
of her	4	0.1%	41
him	4	0.1%	41.3
your eyes	4	0.1%	41.4
i'll	4	0.1%	48.7
we are	4	0.1%	50.3
the light	4	0.1%	52.6

your hands	4	0.1%	54.7
she is	4	0.1%	55.9
i was	4	0.1%	56.2
imagine you	4	0.1%	57.7
red	4	0.1%	59.5
love you	4	0.1%	68
what happens	4	0.1%	71
made me	4	0.1%	71
i've never	4	0.1%	71.5
i don't	4	0.1%	71.5
some days	4	0.1%	72.4
rings and	4	0.1%	78
you get	4	0.1%	78.9
some of	4	0.1%	80.2
don't ever	4	0.1%	80.2
is something	4	0.1%	80.9
ask for	4	0.1%	81
you ask	4	0.1%	81
the door	4	0.1%	86.6
going to	4	0.1%	88.4

being loved	4	0.1%	91.1
thing being	4	0.1%	91.2
brave thing	4	0.1%	91.2
a brave	4	0.1%	91.2
hope of	3	0%	4.6
the hope	3	0%	4.7
you say	3	0%	10.5
skin	3	0%	12.2
for days	3	0%	12.2
pothole is	3	0%	12.3
the pothole	3	0%	12.4
be a	3	0%	13.7
feet	3	0%	14.1
in sand	3	0%	20.1
my dream	3	0%	20.2
wanted to	3	0%	22.2
your voice	3	0%	23.8
mirror	3	0%	24.4
night	3	0%	24.6
time a	3	0%	26.5

with me	3	0%	27.1
my own	3	0%	27.7
i hear	3	0%	28.3
i ll	3	0%	30
or in	3	0%	31.1
into a	3	0%	31.2
don t	3	0%	31.7
it has	3	0%	32.5
my head	3	0%	33.2
naked because	3	0%	34.6
for	3	0%	34.8
in between	3	0%	35
why is	3	0%	35.7
because of	3	0%	36.4
today	3	0%	36.7
me how	3	0%	36.7
talking to	3	0%	37
to my	3	0%	37.3
a small	3	0%	37.7
full of	3	0%	38.3

you are	3	0%	38.8
her poems	3	0%	39
same	3	0%	39.4
the day	3	0%	40.3
listen to	3	0%	40.5
i will	3	0%	40.7
in and	3	0%	40.9
beautiful you	3	0%	42.1
like i	3	0%	42.2
was the	3	0%	42.3
that sounds	3	0%	42.9
have the	3	0%	43.1
what i	3	0%	43.6
to a	3	0%	43.9
blood on	3	0%	44.4
i'd	3	0%	45.7
of love	3	0%	46.6
for me	3	0%	46.8
something that	3	0%	47.3
feet and	3	0%	47.5

your bed	3	0%	47.9
what you	3	0%	48.7
each other	3	0%	48.9
of	3	0%	49.3
you have	3	0%	49.5
until we	3	0%	50.4
you think	3	0%	51.6
eat your	3	0%	51.7
knees	3	0%	51.9
when your	3	0%	52.5
with a	3	0%	52.6
out	3	0%	53.4
up	3	0%	53.7
me a	3	0%	54.7
could be	3	0%	55.4
about you	3	0%	55.7
at me	3	0%	57.4
again in	3	0%	57.5
have been	3	0%	57.6
all things	3	0%	60

to leave	3	0%	60.1
back	3	0%	60.5
there are	3	0%	61.9
for a	3	0%	62
joke is	3	0%	62.4
the joke	3	0%	62.4
the body	3	0%	62.6
to her	3	0%	63
my voice	3	0%	63.3
down to	3	0%	64
of us	3	0%	64.3
i lose	3	0%	64.6
that you	3	0%	65.1
do you	3	0%	66.3
had to	3	0%	67.1
let	3	0%	68.1
as much	3	0%	68.3
tell you	3	0%	68.5
no	3	0%	68.8
me on	3	0%	69.3

belong to	3	0%	69.7
your mouth	3	0%	70
you the	3	0%	70.4
behind me	3	0%	71.3
learned to	3	0%	71.7
i didn't	3	0%	71.9
because	3	0%	72.6
in an	3	0%	72.8
but it's	3	0%	73.8
trying to	3	0%	74.6
on your	3	0%	74.9
wake up	3	0%	75.9
most of	3	0%	76.2
i can	3	0%	76.9
the dreams	3	0%	77
in some	3	0%	77
to stop	3	0%	77.1
call me	3	0%	78.2
bring you	3	0%	79.3
to bring	3	0%	79.3

is for	3	0%	80.2
surprise party	3	0%	81
story	3	0%	82.5
i say	3	0%	83.7
it wasn't	3	0%	84.3
you and	3	0%	90.9
loved by	3	0%	90.9
while you	2	0%	2.4
dear	2	0%	2.6
dear	2	0%	2.6
even	2	0%	4
is always	2	0%	4.4
memory	2	0%	5
said	2	0%	5.6
like spring	2	0%	5.8
lips	2	0%	6.1
are the	2	0%	6.3
hello	2	0%	6.4
you whisper	2	0%	6.7
oh	2	0%	8

daylight	2	0%	8.2
they are	2	0%	8.2
her eyes	2	0%	8.4
over certain	2	0%	9.2
they photograph	2	0%	10.2
never wanted	2	0%	10.3
no you	2	0%	10.3
but no	2	0%	10.3
early	2	0%	11.3
against my	2	0%	11.6
the colour	2	0%	11.6
is my	2	0%	11.6
herself in	2	0%	12.6
thinks herself	2	0%	12.7
the exact	2	0%	12.7
she thinks	2	0%	12.7
texture of	2	0%	12.7
the texture	2	0%	12.7
my memory	2	0%	12.7
sleep and	2	0%	12.9

my body	2	0%	14
rising	2	0%	14.4
holds his	2	0%	14.5
and holds	2	0%	14.5
never gets	2	0%	14.6
but never	2	0%	14.6
smile	2	0%	15.3
old mirror	2	0%	15.5
is old	2	0%	15.5
yesterday is	2	0%	15.5
yesterday	2	0%	15.6
sadness	2	0%	15.6
in sadness	2	0%	15.6
sadness in	2	0%	15.6
is sadness	2	0%	15.6
grief is	2	0%	15.6
a grief	2	0%	15.6
in time	2	0%	15.7
against your	2	0%	15.7
time	2	0%	15.7

is time	2	0%	15.7
ghost is	2	0%	15.7
a ghost	2	0%	15.7
sand a	2	0%	15.7
sand in	2	0%	15.8
is sand	2	0%	15.8
hourglass is	2	0%	15.8
an hourglass	2	0%	15.8
myself	2	0%	15.8
ground myself	2	0%	15.8
i ground	2	0%	15.8
how i	2	0%	15.9
this	2	0%	15.9
early morning	2	0%	15.9
are	2	0%	16.8
my way	2	0%	16.8
at	2	0%	17.6
earth and	2	0%	17.7
morning	2	0%	17.9
i shall	2	0%	18.1

wake to	2	0%	18.7
mine	2	0%	18.8
is	2	0%	19
fingers	2	0%	19
waiting	2	0%	19.9
somewhere in	2	0%	20.1
i would	2	0%	20.3
hear a	2	0%	20.7
the open	2	0%	21.8
watching	2	0%	22
sort of	2	0%	22.1
be alone	2	0%	25
until the	2	0%	25
until	2	0%	25
dream	2	0%	25.8
of me	2	0%	26.1
between	2	0%	26.6
the rain	2	0%	26.6
over the	2	0%	26.9
supposed to	2	0%	27.2

i supposed	2	0%	27.2
my feet	2	0%	27.9
if there	2	0%	28.3
no more	2	0%	28.4
was born	2	0%	28.8
there's no	2	0%	28.9
if there's	2	0%	28.9
of water	2	0%	29
love	2	0%	29.6
me something	2	0%	30.1
sun is	2	0%	30.2
and love	2	0%	30.2
the shadow	2	0%	30.4
that will	2	0%	30.5
again my	2	0%	31
you ever	2	0%	31
have you	2	0%	31
have	2	0%	31
street	2	0%	31.2
with your	2	0%	31.3

me if	2	0%	31.4
t know	2	0%	31.5
root of	2	0%	31.5
the root	2	0%	31.5
what is	2	0%	31.8
your skin	2	0%	32.1
and what	2	0%	32.1
a way	2	0%	32.8
myself to	2	0%	32.9
so you	2	0%	33.2
the moon	2	0%	33.3
winter	2	0%	33.3
thought of	2	0%	33.5
the thought	2	0%	33.5
naked like	2	0%	34
would be	2	0%	34.1
i could	2	0%	34.3
nothing i	2	0%	34.3
was nothing	2	0%	34.3
your life	2	0%	34.4

me to	2	0%	34.4
took my	2	0%	34.4
me in	2	0%	34.4
you took	2	0%	34.4
moon	2	0%	35
not because	2	0%	35.1
clothes	2	0%	35.1
her words	2	0%	35.2
my clothes	2	0%	35.3
what if	2	0%	35.6
see the	2	0%	35.8
leaving	2	0%	35.9
this	2	0%	36.1
with his	2	0%	36.2
i wanted	2	0%	36.2
this time	2	0%	36.4
i touch	2	0%	36.8
or a	2	0%	36.9
why	2	0%	37
by the	2	0%	37.4

a photograph	2	0%	37.6
up to	2	0%	37.8
of you	2	0%	38.1
a star	2	0%	38.2
my teeth	2	0%	38.3
around	2	0%	38.7
you said	2	0%	38.7
nobody will	2	0%	39.2
nobody	2	0%	39.2
a dream	2	0%	39.9
the world	2	0%	39.9
painless	2	0%	40.2
how you	2	0%	40.2
your hand	2	0%	40.3
too	2	0%	40.3
to its	2	0%	40.5
forgiveness	2	0%	41.5
light	2	0%	41.6
about	2	0%	42
nothing to	2	0%	42.3

say nothing	2	0%	42.3
and say	2	0%	42.3
socks	2	0%	42.3
your socks	2	0%	42.3
wear your	2	0%	42.3
sleep in	2	0%	42.4
and sleep	2	0%	42.4
made of	2	0%	42.5
are made	2	0%	42.5
out to	2	0%	42.8
but I	2	0%	42.9
is not	2	0%	43.5
you out	2	0%	43.9
my face	2	0%	44
and made	2	0%	44.3
there would	2	0%	44.6
in bed	2	0%	44.7
how to	2	0%	44.8
under your	2	0%	45.9
always the	2	0%	46.1

cross	2	0%	46.6
eye of	2	0%	46.9
the eye	2	0%	46.9
your name	2	0%	47.1
wall	2	0%	47.2
like to	2	0%	47.2
end of	2	0%	47.3
the end	2	0%	47.3
but she	2	0%	47.4
she doesn't	2	0%	47.5
the faster	2	0%	47.5
under the	2	0%	47.5
sun	2	0%	47.6
the driver	2	0%	47.6
and it	2	0%	47.8
in their	2	0%	47.8
the dark	2	0%	48.3
a rhythm	2	0%	48.6
world and	2	0%	48.6
you had	2	0%	49

my hands	2	0%	49.2
like rain	2	0%	49.2
sounds like	2	0%	49.3
the garden	2	0%	49.3
hour that	2	0%	49.3
an hour	2	0%	49.3
hand in	2	0%	50
the sky	2	0%	50.1
lover was	2	0%	50.1
my lover	2	0%	50.1
if my	2	0%	50.1
of you	2	0%	50.6
to do	2	0%	51.3
early june	2	0%	51.3
to tell	2	0%	51.4
you like	2	0%	51.5
no in	2	0%	52.1
fruit of	2	0%	52.1
ground	2	0%	52.1
the ground	2	0%	52.2

me is	2	0%	52.2
person to	2	0%	52.2
to keep	2	0%	52.5
my eyes	2	0%	53
the train	2	0%	53.1
reflection on	2	0%	53.1
my reflection	2	0%	53.1
meeting my	2	0%	53.1
upon meeting	2	0%	53.2
over a	2	0%	53.2
his eyes	2	0%	53.3
and your	2	0%	53.6
the fire	2	0%	53.9
to jump	2	0%	54.2
of violets	2	0%	54.2
field of	2	0%	54.2
a field	2	0%	54.2
i listen	2	0%	54.5
i'd make	2	0%	54.6
make me	2	0%	54.6

you make	2	0%	54.6
it comes	2	0%	54.7
the dead	2	0%	54.7
the only	2	0%	55.1
the feathers	2	0%	55.2
memory tree	2	0%	55.2
the memory	2	0%	55.2
by a	2	0%	55.4
the mirror	2	0%	55.5
found me	2	0%	55.6
a slow	2	0%	55.7
then I	2	0%	55.9
winter so	2	0%	56
it's winter	2	0%	56
you in	2	0%	56
can find	2	0%	56.1
a little	2	0%	56.3
so beautiful	2	0%	56.4
face	2	0%	56.6
a new	2	0%	56.6

built you	2	0%	56.7
have built	2	0%	56.7
my heart	2	0%	57
if the	2	0%	57.1
about me	2	0%	57.4
heart	2	0%	57.6
time is	2	0%	57.6
taste it	2	0%	57.9
all your	2	0%	57.9
pack my	2	0%	58
let you	2	0%	58.4
it I	2	0%	58.6
a young	2	0%	58.8
at lakeshore	2	0%	59.1
keep your	2	0%	59.4
my shirt	2	0%	59.9
of all	2	0%	60.2
love included	2	0%	60.4
things love	2	0%	60.4
open	2	0%	60.5

the middle	2	0%	60.6
do it	2	0%	60.7
of their	2	0%	60.7
as if	2	0%	60.8
know	2	0%	61.4
side of	2	0%	62
the side	2	0%	62.1
in our	2	0%	62.1
one	2	0%	62.2
the road	2	0%	62.3
moonlight daylight	2	0%	62.4
when they	2	0%	62.6
their feet	2	0%	62.6
the table	2	0%	62.6
in its	2	0%	62.7
of time	2	0%	62.8
down on	2	0%	62.8
get a	2	0%	62.8
but not	2	0%	63.1
early morning	2	0%	63.2

black early	2	0%	63.2
why I	2	0%	63.6
and won't	2	0%	63.6
a river	2	0%	63.7
here	2	0%	63.9
then he	2	0%	63.9
instead of	2	0%	63.9
and then	2	0%	64
you let	2	0%	64.7
many times	2	0%	64.8
so many	2	0%	64.9
here so	2	0%	64.9
been here	2	0%	64.9
we've been	2	0%	64.9
word flow	2	0%	65.2
every time	2	0%	65.5
you back	2	0%	65.9
it doesn't	2	0%	66.1
you turn	2	0%	66.3
get yourself	2	0%	66.4

only way	2	0%	66.5
becomes the	2	0%	66.6
so I	2	0%	67.8
forever vertical	2	0%	68
no no	2	0%	68.8
but most	2	0%	69.1
time you	2	0%	69.3
of course	2	0%	69.4
to love	2	0%	69.7
at least	2	0%	70.6
happens	2	0%	70.6
you what	2	0%	70.6
I'll tell	2	0%	70.6
looking for	2	0%	71.2
happens when	2	0%	71.3
I mean	2	0%	71.3
of birds	2	0%	71.5
destruction of	2	0%	71.5
the destruction	2	0%	71.5
love and	2	0%	71.5

you for	2	0%	71.7
like this	2	0%	71.9
yellow yolk	2	0%	72
sunday's yellow	2	0%	72
is that	2	0%	72.4
matters is	2	0%	72.4
what matters	2	0%	72.5
know what	2	0%	72.7
matter	2	0%	72.9
doesn't matter	2	0%	72.9
so it	2	0%	73
here I	2	0%	73.1
up	2	0%	73.6
wake up	2	0%	73.6
and make	2	0%	73.7
the floor	2	0%	73.9
no one	2	0%	74.3
get to	2	0%	74.6
hallways stretch	2	0%	74.6
the hallways	2	0%	74.6

your smile	2	0%	75
the list	2	0%	75.2
let him	2	0%	75.4
meet again	2	0%	75.4
we	2	0%	75.5
much as	2	0%	75.6
new york	2	0%	75.6
had a	2	0%	75.7
to say	2	0%	76.1
that is	2	0%	76.3
anyway I	2	0%	76.5
it anyway	2	0%	76.5
on it	2	0%	76.5
ketchup on	2	0%	76.6
part of	2	0%	76.6
your heart	2	0%	76.7
did you	2	0%	77.6
you love	2	0%	78.4
for bianca	2	0%	78.4
I kiss	2	0%	78.9

a sound	2	0%	79
the lights	2	0%	79.1
you do	2	0%	79.1
you this	2	0%	80.1
for being	2	0%	80.1
love included	2	0%	80.2
love	2	0%	80.3
I got	2	0%	80.3
the surprise	2	0%	80.6
knees again	2	0%	80.6
so… unexpected	2	0%	80.8
laugh	2	0%	80.8
love is	2	0%	81
please don't	2	0%	81.4
driving into	2	0%	81.5
body made	2	0%	81.8
make excuses	2	0%	82.2
an attempt	2	0%	82.5
got to	2	0%	83.2
I promise	2	0%	83.5

you forget	2	0%	83.6
I knew	2	0%	83.7
holy word	2	0%	83.7
the holy	2	0%	83.7
I like	2	0%	84
I'm sorry	2	0%	84.1
wasn't about	2	0%	84.3
and all	2	0%	84.3
every day	2	0%	84.4
coming	2	0%	84.5
keeps coming	2	0%	84.5
blood keeps	2	0%	84.5
the blood	2	0%	84.5
not you	2	0%	84.6
mouth I	2	0%	84.9
the telephone	2	0%	85
something else	2	0%	85
calls me	2	0%	85
he calls	2	0%	85.1
what happens	2	0%	85.5

the poem	2	0%	85.5
i've tried	2	0%	85.8
my mouth	2	0%	85.9
laugh if	2	0%	86.1
a joke	2	0%	86.1
me but	2	0%	86.1
poem before	2	0%	86.8
this poem	2	0%	86.8
don't ask	2	0%	87.1
same story	2	0%	87.2
know I	2	0%	87.3
it off	2	0%	87.3
cut it	2	0%	87.4
to cut	2	0%	87.4
willing to	2	0%	87.4
someone willing	2	0%	87.4
to someone	2	0%	87.4
your head	2	0%	87.4
bow your	2	0%	87.4
ever bow	2	0%	87.5

him inside	2	0%	87.5
day I	2	0%	88
like that	2	0%	88.2
you with	2	0%	88.3
hurt you	2	0%	88.3
to hurt	2	0%	88.3
i'm going	2	0%	88.3
times i'm	2	0%	88.3
are times	2	0%	88.4
rem sleep	2	0%	88.4
yes there	2	0%	88.4
to bed	2	0%	88.5
the kitchen	2	0%	88.5
god I	2	0%	88.7
been that	2	0%	89
never been	2	0%	89
but then	2	0%	89.1
at all	2	0%	89.3
by me	2	0%	89.9
inside her	2	0%	90

it isn't	2	0%	90.5
some people	2	0%	91.1
we say	2	0%	91.5
re write	2	0%	92.8
where the	2	0%	93.9
poetry is	2	0%	94.1
brave thing	2	0%	95.4
the mountain	2	0%	95.8
los angeles	2	0%	98.5

3 word phrases frequency:

Expression	Count	Frequency	Prominence
I want to	12	0.2%	79.8
we meet again	9	0.1%	51.4
I am naked	6	0.1%	34.5
meet again at	5	0.1%	50.8
the phone rings	5	0.1%	77.9
tell me about	4	0.1%	32.5
phone rings and	4	0.1%	78
you ask for	4	0.1%	81

something you ask	4	0.1%	81
thing being loved	4	0.1%	91.2
brave thing being	4	0.1%	91.2
a brave thing	4	0.1%	91.2
it's a brave	4	0.1%	91.2
the hope of	3	0%	4.6
pothole is a	3	0%	12.3
the pothole is	3	0%	12.3
in my dream	3	0%	20.2
am naked because	3	0%	34.6
why is it	3	0%	35.7
again at the	3	0%	50.4
in the distance	3	0%	54.8
i imagine you	3	0%	57.8
the joke is	3	0%	62.4
of the dreams	3	0%	77
to bring you	3	0%	79.3
is something you	3	0%	81
you and I	3	0%	90.9
being loved by	3	0%	90.9

some days she	3	0%	92.4
you are the	2	0%	6.3
in your voice	2	0%	9.8
wanted to be	2	0%	10.3
never wanted to	2	0%	10.3
you never wanted	2	0%	10.3
no you never	2	0%	10.3
but no you	2	0%	10.3
thinks herself in	2	0%	12.6
she thinks herself	2	0%	12.7
the texture of	2	0%	12.7
in the city	2	0%	12.9
and holds his	2	0%	14.5
but never gets	2	0%	14.6
is old mirror	2	0%	15.5
yesterday is old	2	0%	15.5
sadness yesterday	2	0%	15.6
sadness in sadness	2	0%	15.6
is sadness in	2	0%	15.6
grief is sadness	2	0%	15.6

a grief is	2	0%	15.6
time a grief	2	0%	15.6
in time a	2	0%	15.6
ghost is time	2	0%	15.7
a ghost is	2	0%	15.7
sand a ghost	2	0%	15.7
in sand a	2	0%	15.7
sand in sand	2	0%	15.7
is sand in	2	0%	15.8
hourglass is sand	2	0%	15.8
an hourglass is	2	0%	15.8
i ground myself	2	0%	15.8
how i ground	2	0%	15.8
is how I	2	0%	15.9
this is how	2	0%	15.9
i wake to	2	0%	18.7
somewhere in my	2	0%	20.1
i supposed to	2	0%	27.2
if there's no	2	0%	28.9
tell me something	2	0%	30.1

the sun is	2	0%	30.2
something that will	2	0%	30.5
in my head	2	0%	30.6
have you ever	2	0%	31
me if you	2	0%	31.4
tell me if	2	0%	31.4
the root of	2	0%	31.5
what is the	2	0%	31.7
tell me how	2	0%	32.4
the thought of	2	0%	33.5
am naked like	2	0%	34
nothing I could	2	0%	34.3
was nothing I	2	0%	34.3
there was nothing	2	0%	34.3
you took my	2	0%	34.4
because of the	2	0%	37
on my own	2	0%	37.5
say nothing to	2	0%	42.3
and say nothing	2	0%	42.3
wear your socks	2	0%	42.3

in your bed	2	0%	42.4
sleep in your	2	0%	42.4
and sleep in	2	0%	42.4
are made of	2	0%	42.5
you out of	2	0%	43.8
the eye of	2	0%	46.9
end of the	2	0%	47.3
the end of	2	0%	47.3
there is a	2	0%	47.8
when your eyes	2	0%	47.8
in the dark	2	0%	48.3
the world and	2	0%	48.6
sounds like rain	2	0%	49.3
that sounds like	2	0%	49.3
hour that sounds	2	0%	49.3
an hour that	2	0%	49.3
is an hour	2	0%	49.3
there is an	2	0%	49.3
was the sky	2	0%	50.1
lover was the	2	0%	50.1

my lover was	2	0%	50.1
if my lover	2	0%	50.1
again at a	2	0%	51.4
meet again in	2	0%	51.8
fruit of the	2	0%	52.1
the ground	2	0%	52.1
on the train	2	0%	53.1
reflection on the	2	0%	53.1
my reflection on	2	0%	53.1
meeting my reflection	2	0%	53.1
upon meeting my	2	0%	53.2
and your hands	2	0%	53.6
field of violets	2	0%	54.2
a field of	2	0%	54.2
in a field	2	0%	54.2
i listen to	2	0%	54.5
you make me	2	0%	54.6
when it comes	2	0%	54.7
the memory tree	2	0%	55.2
in your hands	2	0%	55.8

it's winter so	2	0%	56
beautiful you are	2	0%	56.3
so beautiful you	2	0%	56.3
have built you	2	0%	56.7
i have built	2	0%	56.7
want to leave	2	0%	59.5
again in the	2	0%	59.9
things love included	2	0%	60.4
all things love	2	0%	60.4
in the middle	2	0%	60.6
side of your	2	0%	62
the side of	2	0%	62
on the table	2	0%	62.6
black early morning	2	0%	63.2
then he says	2	0%	63.9
and then he	2	0%	63.9
i love you	2	0%	64
so many times	2	0%	64.9
here so many	2	0%	64.9
been here so	2	0%	64.9

we've been here	2	0%	64.9
the only way	2	0%	66.5
but most of	2	0%	69.1
no I	2	0%	69.3
what happens	2	0%	70.6
you what happens	2	0%	70.6
tell you what	2	0%	70.6
i'll tell you	2	0%	70.6
what happens when	2	0%	71.3
what happens	2	0%	71.3
destruction of birds	2	0%	71.5
the destruction of	2	0%	71.5
sunday's yellow yolk	2	0%	72
matters is that	2	0%	72.4
what matters is	2	0%	72.5
what matters	2	0%	72.5
out of your	2	0%	72.9
doesn't matter	2	0%	72.9
and I wake	2	0%	73.6
I wake up	2	0%	73.6

to get to	2	0%	74.6
trying to get	2	0%	74.6
the hallways stretch	2	0%	74.6
we meet again	2	0%	75.4
we meet	2	0%	75.5
much as you	2	0%	75.6
as much as	2	0%	75.6
it anyway I	2	0%	76.5
on it anyway	2	0%	76.5
ketchup on it	2	0%	76.6
I can	2	0%	76.6
this is the	2	0%	76.7
you I don't	2	0%	78.3
all the lights	2	0%	79.1
this is for	2	0%	80
love included	2	0%	80.2
the surprise party	2	0%	80.6
your knees again	2	0%	80.6
to your knees	2	0%	81.3
body made me	2	0%	81.8

your body made	2	0%	81.8
in an attempt	2	0%	82.5
got to go	2	0%	83.2
the holy word	2	0%	83.7
and I say	2	0%	83.7
I like you	2	0%	84
blood keeps coming	2	0%	84.5
the blood keeps	2	0%	84.5
of your body	2	0%	84.9
on the telephone	2	0%	85
me on the	2	0%	85
calls me on	2	0%	85
he calls me	2	0%	85
this poem before	2	0%	86.8
same story	2	0%	87.2
the same story	2	0%	87.2
know I know	2	0%	87.3
cut it off	2	0%	87.4
to cut it	2	0%	87.4
willing to cut	2	0%	87.4

someone willing to	2	0%	87.4
to someone willing	2	0%	87.4
bow your head	2	0%	87.4
ever bow your	2	0%	87.5
hurt you with	2	0%	88.3
to hurt you	2	0%	88.3
going to hurt	2	0%	88.3
I'm going to	2	0%	88.3
times I'm going	2	0%	88.3
are times I'm	2	0%	88.4
there are times	2	0%	88.4
yes there are	2	0%	88.4
going to bed	2	0%	88.5
want to bring	2	0%	88.7
god I want	2	0%	88.7
never been that	2	0%	89
I've never been	2	0%	89
loved by me	2	0%	90

4 word phrases frequency:

Expression	Count	Frequency	Prominence
we meet again at	5	0.1%	50.9
the phone rings and	4	0.1%	78
something you ask for	4	0.1%	81
brave thing being loved	4	0.1%	91.2
a brave thing being	4	0.1%	91.2
it's a brave thing	4	0.1%	91.2
the pothole is a	3	0%	12.3
i am naked because	3	0%	34.6
meet again at the	3	0%	50.4
some of the dreams	3	0%	77
is something you ask	3	0%	81
thing being loved by	3	0%	90.9
never wanted to be	2	0%	10.3
you never wanted to	2	0%	10.3
no you never wanted	2	0%	10.3
but no you never	2	0%	10.3
she thinks herself in	2	0%	12.6
yesterday is old mirror	2	0%	15.5

is sadness in sadness	2	0%	15.6
grief is sadness in	2	0%	15.6
a grief is sadness	2	0%	15.6
time a grief is	2	0%	15.6
in time a grief	2	0%	15.6
a ghost is time	2	0%	15.7
sand a ghost is	2	0%	15.7
in sand a ghost	2	0%	15.7
sand in sand a	2	0%	15.7
is sand in sand	2	0%	15.7
hourglass is sand in	2	0%	15.8
an hourglass is sand	2	0%	15.8
how i ground myself	2	0%	15.8
is how i ground	2	0%	15.8
this is how i	2	0%	15.9
somewhere in my dream	2	0%	20.1
tell me if you	2	0%	31.4
i am naked like	2	0%	34
was nothing i could	2	0%	34.3
there was nothing i	2	0%	34.3

and say nothing to	2	0%	42.3
he'll wear your socks	2	0%	42.3
sleep in your bed	2	0%	42.4
and sleep in your	2	0%	42.4
the end of the	2	0%	47.3
that sounds like rain	2	0%	49.3
hour that sounds like	2	0%	49.3
an hour that sounds	2	0%	49.3
is an hour that	2	0%	49.3
there is an hour	2	0%	49.3
lover was the sky	2	0%	50.1
my lover was the	2	0%	50.1
if my lover was	2	0%	50.1
meet again at a	2	0%	51.4
we meet again in	2	0%	51.8
reflection on the train	2	0%	53.1
my reflection on the	2	0%	53.1
meeting my reflection on	2	0%	53.1
upon meeting my reflection		2	0%	53.1
a field of violets	2	0%	54.2

in a field of	2	0%	54.2
so beautiful you are	2	0%	56.3
i have built you	2	0%	56.7
all things love included	2	0%	60.4
the side of your	2	0%	62
and then he says	2	0%	63.9
here so many times	2	0%	64.9
been here so many	2	0%	64.9
we've been here so	2	0%	64.9
tell you what happens	2	0%	70.6
i'll tell you what	2	0%	70.6
the destruction of birds	2	0%	71.5
what matters is that	2	0%	72.5
trying to get to	2	0%	74.6
as much as you	2	0%	75.6
on it anyway I	2	0%	76.5
ketchup on it anyway	2	0%	76.6
your body made me	2	0%	81.8
the blood keeps coming	2	0%	84.5
me on the telephone	2	0%	85

calls me on the	2	0%	85
he calls me on	2	0%	85
to cut it off	2	0%	87.4
willing to cut it	2	0%	87.4
someone willing to cut	2	0%	87.4
to someone willing to	2	0%	87.4
ever bow your head	2	0%	87.5
to hurt you with	2	0%	88.3
going to hurt you	2	0%	88.3
i'm going to hurt	2	0%	88.3
times i'm going to	2	0%	88.3
are times i'm going	2	0%	88.4
there are times i'm	2	0%	88.4
yes there are times	2	0%	88.4
want to bring you	2	0%	88.7
I want to bring	2	0%	88.7
god I want to	2	0%	88.7
I've never been that	2	0%	89
being loved by me	2	0%	90

word phrases frequency:

Expression	Count	Frequency	Prominence
a brave thing being loved	4	0.1%	91.2
it's a brave thing being	4	0.1%	91.2
we meet again at the	3	0%	50.4
in some of the dreams	3	0%	77
is something you ask for	3	0%	81
brave thing being loved by	3	0%	91
you never wanted to be	2	0%	10.3
no you never wanted to	2	0%	10.3
but no you never wanted	2	0%	10.3
grief is sadness in sadness	2	0%	15.6
a grief is sadness in	2	0%	15.6
time a grief is sadness	2	0%	15.6
in time a grief is	2	0%	15.6
sand a ghost is time	2	0%	15.7
in sand a ghost is	2	0%	15.7
sand in sand a ghost	2	0%	15.7
is sand in sand a	2	0%	15.7
hourglass is sand in sand	2	0%	15.7

an hourglass is sand in	2	0%	15.8	
an hourglass is sand	2	0%	15.8	
myself an hourglass is	2	0%	15.8	
ground myself an hourglass		2	0%	15.8
is how i ground myself	2	0%	15.8	
there was nothing i could	2	0%	34.3	
and sleep in your bed	2	0%	42.4	
hour that sounds like rain	2	0%	49.3	
an hour that sounds like	2	0%	49.3	
is an hour that sounds	2	0%	49.3	
there is an hour that	2	0%	49.3	
my lover was the sky	2	0%	50.1	
if my lover was the	2	0%	50.1	
we meet again at a	2	0%	51.5	
my reflection on the train	2	0%	53.1	
meeting my reflection on the		2	0%	53.1
upon meeting my reflection on		2	0%	53.1
in a field of violets	2	0%	54.2	
all things love included	2	0%	60.4	
been here so many times	2	0%	64.9	

we've been here so many	2	0%	64.9
tell you what happens	2	0%	70.6
i'll tell you what happens	2	0%	70.6
calls me on the telephone	2	0%	85
he calls me on the	2	0%	85
willing to cut it off	2	0%	87.4
someone willing to cut it	2	0%	87.4
to someone willing to cut	2	0%	87.4
going to hurt you with	2	0%	88.3
i'm going to hurt you	2	0%	88.3
times i'm going to hurt	2	0%	88.3
are times i'm going to	2	0%	88.4
there are times i'm going	2	0%	88.4
yes there are times i'm	2	0%	88.4
i want to bring you	2	0%	88.7
god i want to bring	2	0%	88.7
thing being loved by me	2	0%	90

Unfiltered word count :

Expression	Count	Frequency	Prominence
the	360	4.5%	49.8
i	181	2.3%	55.1
of	173	2.2%	46.8
a	166	2.1%	46.1
you	161	2%	54.7
to	157	2%	57.1
and	151	1.9%	48.8
in	146	1.8%	40.7
your	101	1.3%	51.2
my	91	1.1%	42.4
is	88	1.1%	44.2
me	74	0.9%	51.8
it	69	0.9%	61.4
on	54	0.7%	44.3
like	47	0.6%	48.9
with	43	0.5%	47.3
for	41	0.5%	54.5

that	40	0.5%	57.4
her	36	0.5%	43.7
at	36	0.5%	52.6
but	33	0.4%	59.2
we	31	0.4%	57.7
all	31	0.4%	68.1
she	29	0.4%	38.8
or	28	0.4%	46.6
no	28	0.4%	49.2
are	26	0.3%	39.4
he	26	0.3%	46.8
have	26	0.3%	48.2
love	26	0.3%	59
when	24	0.3%	49.1
so	24	0.3%	54.1
what	24	0.3%	57
as	23	0.3%	48.1
there	22	0.3%	38.1
into	22	0.3%	47.1
out	22	0.3%	54.5

this	22	0.3%	55.2
if	21	0.3%	40.9
time	21	0.3%	42.3
from	21	0.3%	46.3
by	21	0.3%	51.9
it's	20	0.3%	77.5
about	19	0.2%	39.8
was	19	0.2%	41.9
something	19	0.2%	63.6
tell	18	0.2%	41.8
be	18	0.2%	44.3
one	18	0.2%	52.8
get	17	0.2%	68.3
an	16	0.2%	47.1
because	16	0.2%	52.5
way	15	0.2%	37.6
our	15	0.2%	47
again	15	0.2%	53.6
not	15	0.2%	56.4
want	15	0.2%	74

they	14	0.2%	35.5
how	14	0.2%	39
never	14	0.2%	50.4
know	14	0.2%	65
will	13	0.2%	40
meet	13	0.2%	53.5
up	13	0.2%	61.3
down	13	0.2%	61.4
body	13	0.2%	72.1
feet	12	0.2%	39.9
his	12	0.2%	40.6
say	12	0.2%	58.5
made	12	0.2%	65.5
don't	12	0.2%	73.4
some	12	0.2%	74.1
eyes	11	0.1%	37.3
between	11	0.1%	45
only	11	0.1%	55
make	11	0.1%	56.2
their	11	0.1%	57.3

before	11	0.1%	60.6
always	10	0.1%	33.8
around	10	0.1%	36
days	10	0.1%	37.2
am	10	0.1%	39.6
bed	10	0.1%	50.7
hands	10	0.1%	53.8
him	10	0.1%	58.4
had	10	0.1%	65.2
do	10	0.1%	67.6
I'm	10	0.1%	84.5
city	9	0.1%	19.3
skin	9	0.1%	20.7
under	9	0.1%	34.1
too	9	0.1%	35.2
other	9	0.1%	45.5
now	9	0.1%	46.5
where	9	0.1%	53.7
day	9	0.1%	54.1
same	9	0.1%	57

been	9	0.1%	61.5
heart	9	0.1%	61.9
off	9	0.1%	66.2
them	9	0.1%	68.1
here	9	0.1%	68.2
knees	9	0.1%	71.6
I've	9	0.1%	79.6
against	8	0.1%	10.6
night	8	0.1%	22.3
over	8	0.1%	31.2
naked	8	0.1%	32.2
while	8	0.1%	35.3
until	8	0.1%	35.6
light	8	0.1%	37.5
each	8	0.1%	42
its	8	0.1%	45.7
could	8	0.1%	48.6
nothing	8	0.1%	50.1
us	8	0.1%	54.7
has	8	0.1%	58.1

much	8	0.1%	59.4
imagine	8	0.1%	61.3
let	8	0.1%	63.5
ever	8	0.1%	63.7
can	8	0.1%	66.4
every	8	0.1%	67.6
you're	8	0.1%	68
mouth	8	0.1%	73.1
keep	8	0.1%	74
memory	7	0.1%	21.4
morning	7	0.1%	24.6
sadness	7	0.1%	28.9
dream	7	0.1%	29.8
world	7	0.1%	41.3
you	7	0.1%	43.9
words	7	0.1%	48.1
left	7	0.1%	51.7
red	7	0.1%	51.9
me	7	0.1%	52.4
find	7	0.1%	52.5

blood	7	0.1%	53.1
head	7	0.1%	55.2
face	7	0.1%	58.1
then	7	0.1%	58.8
wake	7	0.1%	58.9
I'll	7	0.1%	62.4
still	7	0.1%	67.7
just	7	0.1%	67.8
doesn't	7	0.1%	68
ask	7	0.1%	79.4
brave	7	0.1%	80.8
sand	6	0.1%	16.6
today	6	0.1%	25.1
even	6	0.1%	25.6
last	6	0.1%	34
hear	6	0.1%	36
ground	6	0.1%	36.5
watch	6	0.1%	37.8
early	6	0.1%	43.5
voice	6	0.1%	43.5

why	6	0.1%	44.5
who	6	0.1%	50.3
dreams	6	0.1%	50.4
small	6	0.1%	52.8
shirt	6	0.1%	52.8
things	6	0.1%	56.1
gets	6	0.1%	56.8
back	6	0.1%	57.8
think	6	0.1%	58.5
yourself	6	0.1%	59
leave	6	0.1%	63.5
go	6	0.1%	68.3
poetry	6	0.1%	68.4
going	6	0.1%	71.4
says	6	0.1%	72.1
people	6	0.1%	73.1
thing	6	0.1%	76.7
being	6	0.1%	87.5
herself	5	0.1%	14.2
darkness	5	0.1%	15.8

rising	5	0.1%	19.1
thought	5	0.1%	23.6
earth	5	0.1%	25
full	5	0.1%	31
hair	5	0.1%	31.9
little	5	0.1%	32.9
mirror	5	0.1%	34.2
moon	5	0.1%	35.1
more	5	0.1%	35.9
sun	5	0.1%	36.1
thought	5	0.1%	37.5
look	5	0.1%	40.1
winter	5	0.1%	40.1
eat	5	0.1%	40.3
everything	5	0.1%	40.7
through	5	0.1%	41.1
star	5	0.1%	42.8
sleep	5	0.1%	42.8
remember	5	0.1%	45.3
open	5	0.1%	45.6

word	5	0.1%	45.8
forget	5	0.1%	46.8
behind	5	0.1%	51.8
i'd	5	0.1%	51.9
two	5	0.1%	52.8
sometimes	5	0.1%	52.9
god	5	0.1%	54.6
came	5	0.1%	54.7
after	5	0.1%	56.4
turn	5	0.1%	56.6
come	5	0.1%	56.6
someone	5	0.1%	57.6
were	5	0.1%	58.4
can't	5	0.1%	59
wear	5	0.1%	60.6
born	5	0.1%	61.5
stop	5	0.1%	67.7
three	5	0.1%	67.8
writing	5	0.1%	69.9
joke	5	0.1%	71.9

loved	5	0.1%	74.6
holy	5	0.1%	74.8
rings	5	0.1%	77.9
phone	5	0.1%	77.9
kiss	5	0.1%	80.6
laugh	5	0.1%	82.4
inside	5	0.1%	83.7
door	5	0.1%	86.6
hope	4	0.1%	4.8
thinks	4	0.1%	13.1
grey	4	0.1%	19.7
above	4	0.1%	20.7
wanted	4	0.1%	23.3
photograph	4	0.1%	23.9
myself	4	0.1%	24.4
water	4	0.1%	27.7
life	4	0.1%	29.6
streets	4	0.1%	30.1
dark	4	0.1%	31.6
room	4	0.1%	32.4

would	4	0.1%	32.4
fall	4	0.1%	33.8
warm	4	0.1%	35
clothes	4	0.1%	35.2
said	4	0.1%	36.6
name	4	0.1%	37.8
touch	4	0.1%	38.1
old	4	0.1%	38.7
shadow	4	0.1%	39.3
end	4	0.1%	40.9
love	4	0.1%	41.9
keeps	4	0.1%	44.3
side	4	0.1%	45.1
smile	4	0.1%	45.1
breath	4	0.1%	45.4
wall	4	0.1%	46.1
bright	4	0.1%	46.9
moonlight	4	0.1%	47.5
sleep	4	0.1%	50.6
there's	4	0.1%	51.4

moment	4	0.1%	51.4
cry	4	0.1%	52.3
good	4	0.1%	56.2
tongue	4	0.1%	57.1
built	4	0.1%	57.3
looking	4	0.1%	57.8
table	4	0.1%	59.3
lights	4	0.1%	59.4
distance	4	0.1%	59.8
bring	4	0.1%	61.3
we're	4	0.1%	61.7
cut	4	0.1%	63.6
hand	4	0.1%	63.8
learned	4	0.1%	65.1
another	4	0.1%	67.1
both	4	0.1%	67.7
any	4	0.1%	68.1
surprise	4	0.1%	68.4
becomes	4	0.1%	68.8
happens	4	0.1%	71

most	4	0.1%	71.9
trying	4	0.1%	72
well	4	0.1%	73
party	4	0.1%	73.4
new	4	0.1%	75.6
times	4	0.1%	76.6
need	4	0.1%	79.4
story	4	0.1%	81.5
got	4	0.1%	81.7
call	4	0.1%	82.1
anyway	4	0.1%	82.3
wasn't	4	0.1%	84.3
sorry	4	0.1%	85.2
poem	4	0.1%	86.2
lips	3	0%	6.3
laughter	3	0%	9.1
daylight	3	0%	10.2
toes	3	0%	10.5
pothole	3	0%	12.4
fog	3	0%	12.6

grief	3	0%	14.1
dawn	3	0%	14.2
leaves	3	0%	20.3
falling	3	0%	20.6
curled	3	0%	22.3
root	3	0%	24.7
exact	3	0%	26
rain	3	0%	27.1
somewhere	3	0%	27.7
shoulders	3	0%	27.7
own	3	0%	27.7
certain	3	0%	27.9
float	3	0%	28.6
teeth	3	0%	29.8
mine	3	0%	30.4
don	3	0%	31.7
hour	3	0%	33.1
thoughts	3	0%	34.5
see	3	0%	36.4
talking	3	0%	37

out	3	0%	37.4
train	3	0%	37.4
broken	3	0%	38.1
are	3	0%	38.8
poems	3	0%	38.9
long	3	0%	40
young	3	0%	40.1
listen	3	0%	40.5
beautiful	3	0%	42.1
fire	3	0%	42.5
sounds	3	0%	42.9
took	3	0%	42.9
comes	3	0%	43.8
only	3	0%	45.3
faster	3	0%	45.9
write	3	0%	46.7
upon	3	0%	48.1
yellow	3	0%	49.3
gold	3	0%	49.6
dead	3	0%	49.6

laughing	3	0%	50
again	3	0%	51.5
far	3	0%	51.7
folding	3	0%	52.7
reflection	3	0%	54.4
stretch	3	0%	54.6
feathers	3	0%	55.7
went	3	0%	56.3
slow	3	0%	56.6
crying	3	0%	57.6
kind	3	0%	58.4
real	3	0%	59.6
green	3	0%	59.9
did	3	0%	60.4
taken	3	0%	61
wouldn't	3	0%	61.3
self	3	0%	61.7
wooden	3	0%	62.4
wanting	3	0%	62.5
longer	3	0%	63

person	3	0%	64.4
understand	3	0%	64.6
lose	3	0%	64.6
falls	3	0%	64.8
found	3	0%	66.3
won't	3	0%	67.2
part	3	0%	67.6
home	3	0%	67.8
help	3	0%	67.9
spend	3	0%	69.3
belong	3	0%	69.7
didn't	3	0%	71.9
written	3	0%	73
course	3	0%	74.1
without	3	0%	75.7
forever	3	0%	75.8
mean	3	0%	76.9
getting	3	0%	78.2
except	3	0%	79.7
else	3	0%	80.2

yes	3	0%	81.2
sound	3	0%	82.3
really	3	0%	83.5
first	3	0%	84.4
okay	3	0%	85.5
close	3	0%	87.7
dear	2	0%	2.6
sunset	2	0%	5.3
spring	2	0%	5.8
fingers	2	0%	6.3
hello	2	0%	6.4
whisper	2	0%	6.7
cool	2	0%	7
elsewhere	2	0%	7.9
oh	2	0%	8
afternoon	2	0%	8.9
growing	2	0%	9.1
remembers	2	0%	9.2
horizon	2	0%	9.7
lungs	2	0%	10.3

solitary	2	0%	11.6
colour	2	0%	11.6
midday	2	0%	11.9
creases	2	0%	12.4
texture	2	0%	12.7
these	2	0%	13.9
body	2	0%	14
slips	2	0%	14.4
holds	2	0%	14.5
cup	2	0%	14.6
window	2	0%	15
show	2	0%	15.2
yesterday	2	0%	15.6
ghost	2	0%	15.7
hourglass	2	0%	15.8
veins	2	0%	15.9
ring	2	0%	16.9
melting	2	0%	17
sweater	2	0%	17.7
them	2	0%	17.8

shall	2	0%	18.1
fingers	2	0%	19
waiting	2	0%	19.9
lakeshore	2	0%	20
near	2	0%	21.2
trace	2	0%	21.7
watching	2	0%	22
fear	2	0%	22
sort	2	0%	22.1
mirrors	2	0%	22.6
carry	2	0%	22.8
roots	2	0%	24.3
late	2	0%	24.4
alone	2	0%	25
sky	2	0%	25
cream	2	0%	26.3
someday	2	0%	26.3
sea	2	0%	26.8
supposed	2	0%	27.2
bitter	2	0%	27.2

than	2	0%	27.3
rest	2	0%	27.5
myself	2	0%	27.9
yet	2	0%	28.7
child	2	0%	30.7
wrap	2	0%	30.8
sit	2	0%	30.8
couldn't	2	0%	30.9
hold	2	0%	31
street	2	0%	31.2
seen	2	0%	31.4
heavy	2	0%	31.4
know	2	0%	31.5
station	2	0%	31.7
money	2	0%	31.7
stories	2	0%	32.1
us	2	0%	32.3
steam	2	0%	32.6
works	2	0%	32.7
heat	2	0%	33

years	2	0%	33.9
often	2	0%	34
might	2	0%	34.8
that	2	0%	35
cat	2	0%	35.4
leaving	2	0%	35.9
person	2	0%	36.5
together	2	0%	36.6
white	2	0%	36.8
bus	2	0%	36.8
power	2	0%	37.2
spot	2	0%	38.3
deep	2	0%	38.3
nobody	2	0%	39.2
intent	2	0%	39.5
everywhere	2	0%	39.7
world	2	0%	39.9
painless	2	0%	40.2
cheek	2	0%	40.4
him	2	0%	40.4

themselves	2	0%	41.4
forgiveness	2	0%	41.5
weight	2	0%	41.8
pillow	2	0%	42.1
swallow	2	0%	42.2
words	2	0%	42.3
socks	2	0%	42.3
away	2	0%	42.4
meant	2	0%	43.3
curve	2	0%	43.4
candle	2	0%	43.6
dinner	2	0%	45
hours	2	0%	45.3
to	2	0%	45.6
dust	2	0%	46.5
cross	2	0%	46.6
anything	2	0%	46.8
eye	2	0%	46.9
children	2	0%	47.6
driver	2	0%	47.6

\

though	2	0%	47.6
rhythm	2	0%	48.6
high	2	0%	48.6
rain	2	0%	49.2
garden	2	0%	49.3
daily	2	0%	49.3
shaking	2	0%	49.3
sky	2	0%	50.1
lover	2	0%	50.1
raised	2	0%	50.2
bad	2	0%	50.3
june	2	0%	51.3
endless	2	0%	51.5
fruit	2	0%	52.1
waking	2	0%	52.3
enough	2	0%	52.5
bridge	2	0%	52.6
train	2	0%	53.1
meeting	2	0%	53.2
pass	2	0%	53.8

met	2	0%	54	
drag	2	0%	54.1	
wallflower	2	0%	54.1	
jump	2	0%	54.2	
violets	2	0%	54.2	
field	2	0%	54.2	
origami	2	0%	54.6	
fell	2	0%	54.7	
loneliness	2	0%	54.7	
wet	2	0%	54.9	
tree	2	0%	55.2	
wish	2	0%	55.7	
supermarket	2	0%	55.8	
fast	2	0%	56.1	
milk	2	0%	56.2	
imagined	2	0%	56.6	
relationships	2	0%	56.7	
purple	2	0%	56.7	
breathturn	2	0%	57.2	
next	2	0%	57.5	

spent	2	0%	57.6
taste	2	0%	57.9
pack	2	0%	58
inpatience	2	0%	58
change	2	0%	58.4
conviction	2	0%	58.7
begin	2	0%	58.8
lakeshore	2	0%	59
mind	2	0%	60.1
review	2	0%	60.4
hairbrush	2	0%	60.4
included	2	0%	60.4
goose	2	0%	60.5
middle	2	0%	60.5
they're	2	0%	60.9
deaf	2	0%	61.2
ends	2	0%	61.6
wait	2	0%	61.6
feel	2	0%	61.6
happy	2	0%	61.9

thoughts	2	0%		62.1
road	2	0%	62.2	
survival	2	0%	62.3	
daylight	2	0%	62.4	
leaning	2	0%	62.7	
kisses	2	0%	62.8	
morning	2	0%		63.2
black	2	0%	63.2	
houses	2	0%	63.6	
fries	2	0%	63.6	
river	2	0%	63.7	
instead	2	0%	63.9	
screaming	2	0%		64.3
many	2	0%	64.8	
we've	2	0%	64.9	
flow	2	0%	65.2	
fairy	2	0%	65.3	
grass	2	0%	65.3	
eyes	2	0%	65.3	
season	2	0%	65.6	

spilled	2	0%	66.2
newborns	2	0%	66.2
turning	2	0%	66.5
beer	2	0%	67
one	2	0%	67.3
lonely	2	0%	67.4
spill	2	0%	67.8
vertical	2	0%	68
hanging	2	0%	68
top	2	0%	68.1
tenuous	2	0%	69.2
try	2	0%	69.3
d	2	0%	69.4
live	2	0%	69.8
she's	2	0%	69.8
ghost	2	0%	70.4
that's	2	0%	70.5
least	2	0%	70.6
finally	2	0%	70.6
salvation	2	0%	71

hate	2	0%	71.1	
collection	2	0%	71.3
birds	2	0%	71.4	
destruction	2	0%	71.5
yolk	2	0%	72	
sunday's	2	0%	72	
you'd	2	0%	72.1	
matters	2	0%	72.5	
silence	2	0%	72.6	
dress	2	0%	72.7	
matter	2	0%	72.9	
up	2	0%	73.6	
floor	2	0%	73.9	
aren't	2	0%	74	
man	2	0%	74.6	
run	2	0%	74.6	
hallways	2	0%	74.6	
list	2	0%	75.2	
paper	2	0%	75.5	
york	2	0%	75.6	

book	2	0%	76.3
ketchup	2	0%	76.6
shows	2	0%	77.1
very	2	0%	78.2
bianca	2	0%	78.4
'surprise	2	0%	79.3
included	2	0%	80.2
unexpected	2	0%	80.8
so...	2	0%	80.8
you've	2	0%	81.4
please	2	0%	81.4
driving	2	0%	81.5
apocalypse	2	0%	81.6
excuses	2	0%	82.2
read	2	0%	82.2
attempt	2	0%	82.5
art	2	0%	82.7
form	2	0%	83.2
dresses	2	0%	83.3
quote	2	0%	83.3

Word				
good	2	0%	83.4	
promise	2	0%	83.5	
blame	2	0%	83.5	
goes	2	0%	83.6	
knew	2	0%	83.7	
let's	2	0%	83.7	
word	2	0%	83.7	
bacon	2	0%	84.3	
coming	2	0%	84.5	
women	2	0%	84.6	
telephone	2	0%		85
calls	2	0%	85	
someone's	2	0%		85.3
happens	2	0%	85.5	
tried	2	0%	85.7	
whatever	2	0%		87.3
willing	2	0%	87.4	
bow	2	0%	87.5	
woman	2	0%	88.3	
hurt	2	0%	88.3	

rem	2	0%	88.4
kitchen	2	0%	88.5
dance	2	0%	89.9
maybe	2	0%	90
lost	2	0%	90
knees	2	0%	90.3
isn't	2	0%	90.5
right	2	0%	91.8
write	2	0%	92.8
thing	2	0%	95.3
mountain	2	0%	95.8
charm	2	0%	96
means	2	0%	96.7

2014 Releases

RED PAINT HILL

Please visit www.redpainthill.com for catalogue information, updates, Red Paint Hill Poetry Journal and more.

Also, find us on Facebook: https://www.facebook.com/redpainthill Twitter: https://twitter.com/RedPaintHill Tumblr: http://redpainthill.tumblr.com/

"This city is a lady with a littered heart
and a drunken locksmith for a father."

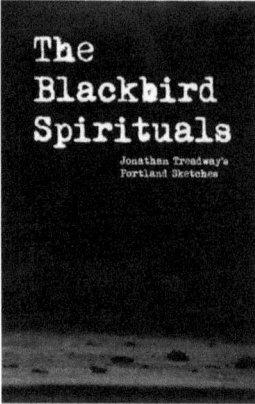

The
Blackbird
Spirituals
Jonathan Treadway's
Portland Sketches

The Blackbird Spirituals poems
are sad bastard poems, poems about
longing, poems about place, and
being misplaced. Treadway opens
his guts and pours them into a
finely tuned book of poems and
postcards.

Treadway is a Kentucky mystic. Singing old harp hymns and
casting chicken bones on a plank floor. In *The Blackbird
Spirituals* he takes that seer's eye and trains it on Portland and
tells it like it is in a voice as universal as... the gospel itself:
Heavy enough so that the best-read intellectual can drink his
fill, and simple enough so that the small child can dip down
and take a drink of water. It's the roar of the Pacific Ocean and
the whisper of mountain streams. It's full emersion and infant
baptism. It's the Lion of the Tribe of Judah and a lamb that
was slain. Reading *The Blackbird Spirituals* is like church, or
like how church was always supposed to be.

– Verless Doran, American poet

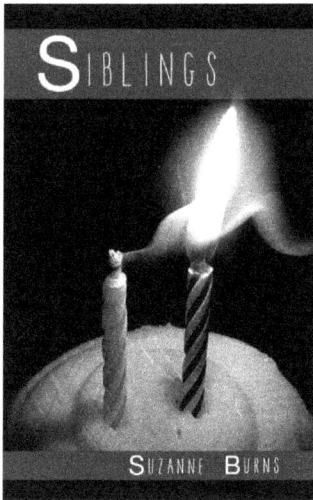

Siblings is the 2013 DIAGRAM Innovative Fiction Contest winner, selected by judge Ben Marcus, who had this to say about the story:

Suzanne Burns has perfectly captured the powerful strangeness of childhood, the fear and joy and weird rituals we invent to work out our place in the world.

She is a visionary poet, with an imagination I'd kill for, and in *Siblings* she's written a piece of otherworldly, mythic sorrow.

Get ready to blast through the haunted back alleys and front doors of the past. Powerful, inimitable, and unforgettable!

—Meg Tuite

Also available at
Powell's Books
1005 W Burnside St.
Portland, OR 97209
503-228-4651
9:00 a.m. - 11:00 p.m.

Windsock Etiquette is moonlight on the porches of Pennsylvania mill towns, but like Berrigan it wears its heart on its blue collar and yearns for simplicity in an age where everything seems so damned complicated. This book is love poems, death poems, songs of potential and broken promise--it takes urban culture back to nature and redefines Americana in a time when we're still very much searching for ourselves.

- John Dorsey, American poet & playwright

In the same way I'm drawn to a Terrance Malick film, a Miles Davis record, an ink blot Rorschach test, I'm drawn towards *Windsock Etiquette*, the collection of linked free-form sonnets by Zach Fishel, spanning across 52 pieces without title, without pandering or any other fence posts to hang a lantern to light one's path through the verse.

This is an adventurous work, where all poems communicate with each other in a resounding way, revealing each strand heartbeat by heartbeat. It feels like a random car ride west across America, searching for gas station coffee, tuning the radio randomly and gathering clips of beautiful info.

-Bud Smith, writer, reviewer

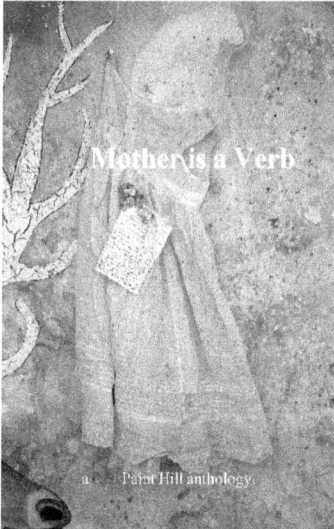

The poems in *Mother is a Verb* reveal a very forthright study of who our mothers really are. After reflecting on the mother-relationship, I decided that we all have intensely strong thoughts about our mothers, grandmothers, or anyone else who became our mother figure. These can either be positive or negative. At some point in our lives, by pinpointing who our mother figure really is/was internally, we then can begin to understand our own flaws, our own talents, and our inner voice. Mother is not just a word, but it is movement, it is action. Mother is our future and our past. Mother....does. Mother...is.

Cover Artwork: Alexandra Eldridge

Contributors include: David Ebenbach, Jennifer Givhan, LS Bassen, Brian Bodeur, Kiley Cogis Brodeur, Alyssa Yankwitt, Hedwika Cox, Bree A Rofle, Steve Brightman, Zach Fishel, Nandini Dhar, Claudia Serea, MJ Iuppa, James Sanchez, Heather Minette, Andrea Rogers, Alicia Elkort, Tracy Davidson, Autumn Konopka, Michael Mark, Mary Lou Buschi, Laurie Jean Cannady, Nicole Caruso Garcia, Jay Sizemore, Brian Patrick Heston, Abigail Wyatt, Telaina Eriksen, Ian Spiegel-Blum

John Swain's *Ring the Sycamore Sky* can maybe be described in terms of what light would do to the earth if there was no night to bestow on it.

His words envision a sacred nature where animals and the living creatures beyond the piles of raw vegetation of the wild can possess or address the mystery of life commanded by different sources of light, among which, love is the most sought after.

-Marlena Bontas

Every word from Swain beguiles the audience, and like Italo Calvino's *Upon A Winter's Night A Traveler*, the reader falls in love with the author, soaking up the sunshine of each expression, taken in by the easily digested themes, the stark imagery, and the rhythmic rapture as "the sun scorched hill touched our backs\ beneath the golden talons of a closer sky."

-Elizabeth Mobley

The Autism Foundation of Tennessee

Karen and Steve Blake founded the Autism Foundation of Tennessee to help families receive therapy and support needed at the lowest possible cost. Karen has a Master's degree in Special Education and Speech-Language Pathology. She also worked 11 years in the public school systems in Atlanta before having a child with Autism.

After experiencing the intensive therapy and the cost associated with it, she realized the need for a non-profit organization to help raise money and to provide individualized programs and services for children with autism and related disorders in Tennessee. The AFT helps children of all ages and will be expanding soon to offer even more services.

The Autism Foundation of TN offers a full range of services for children and adolescents. Some of the targeted skills include: Behavior therapy, Communication, Self-help Skills, Academics, Socialization, Vocational skills, and Family and School Support. The AFT works collaboratively with school systems, and other professionals.

Services Available:
Speech Therapy
Occupational Therapy
ABA Therapy
Social Skills Group
Training and Support

For more information about The Autism Foundation of TN
www.autismfoundationtn.org

www.ingramcontent.com/pod-product-compliance
Lightning Source LLC
Chambersburg PA
CBHW060207070426
42447CB00035B/2791